Loving Within:

A RECOVERY MANUAL

JEREMY HUTCHINS

Ⓟ A PLUME BOOK

PLUME

Published by The Penguin Group

Penguin Group (USA) Inc., 375 Hudson Street, New York, NY 10014 U.S.A.

Penguin Books Ltd. 80 Strand, London WC2R ORL, England

Penguin Books Australia Ltd. 250 Camberwell Road, Victoria 3124, Australia

Penguin Books Canada Ltd. 10 Alcorn Avenue, Toronto, Ontario, Canada M4V 3B2

Penguin Books India (P) Ltd, 11 Community Centre, Panchsheel Park, New Delhi - 110 017 India

Penguin Books (NZ), CNR Airborne and Rosedale Roads, Albany, Auckland 1310, New Zealand

Penguin Books (South Africa) (Pty) Ltd, 24 Sturdee Avenue, Rose Bank, Johannesburg 2196, South Africa

Penguin Books Ltd., Registered offices: 80 Strand, London WC2R ORL England

First published by Plume, a member of Penguin Group (USA) Inc.

First Printing, July 2004

10 9 8 7 6 5 4 3 2 1

Ⓟ Registered Trademark - Marca Registrada

ISBN 0-452-28625-5

Printed in the United States of America

LET'S FACE IT...

DEEP DOWN INSIDE
EACH AND EVERY ONE OF US,
THERE'S A LITTLE
DICK CHENEY
LURKING WITHIN...

DO YOU EVER
HAVE A SECRET DESIRE
TO
CONTROL
THE WORLD?

DO YOU EVER

WANT TO

- wreck a national forest?
- rip off an old lady?
- poison a stream?
- steal candy from a child?

ROB THE COUNTRY BLIND?

When You're Asleep at Night,

do you GRIND YOUR TEETH
and nurse MALICIOUS THOUGHTS
and ANCIENT GRIEVANCES
against the human race?

ARE THERE NEO CONS BREEDING IN YOUR BATHROOM?

ARE YOU

UNABLE TO IDENTIFY

AND EXPRESS

FEELINGS?

ARE YOU AN ENABLER?

ENABLING IS A DYSFUNCTIONAL BEHAVIOR PATTERN IN WHICH THE SURVIVOR BELIEVES HE CAN MAINTAIN RELATIONSHIPS THROUGH

MANIPULATION and CONTROL.

ARE SUSPICIONS
MULTIPLYING IN YOUR
MIND
LIKE LOCUSTS?

ARE YOU ADDICTED TO SECRECY AND POWER? Do you try to FILL YOUR INNER HUNGER WITH MONEY AND FOOD?

HAVE YOU WORKED YOUR BRAIN INTO AN IMPOSSIBLE CRYPTIC KNOT?

IS YOUR BIONIC HEART

FILLED WITH CORRUPTION?

COUNTER SURVEILLANCE

SHIFTY EYES

MALEVOLENT SNEER

BLOOD REPLACED BY DEPLETED URANIUM

MALICIOUS THOUGHTS PLANS AND PREPARATIONS

CURIOUS ABSENCE OF NECK

SECRET CHAMBER

"HEART" MADE BY PARTS OF MISSILE BUILT BY LOCKHEED MARTIN

ILL WILL

DO YOU FIND YOURSELF SKULKING AROUND STREET CORNERS, LOOKING OUT FOR YOUR ENEMIES?

HAVE YOU BEEN
WON OVER
BY THE
DARKER FORCES?

THEY'RE
TERRIBLE
THOUGHTS...
YOU WISH YOU NEVER HAD 'EM
BUT... WELL...**THERE THEY ARE**
YOU DIDN'T **CHOOSE** TO HAVE THEM.

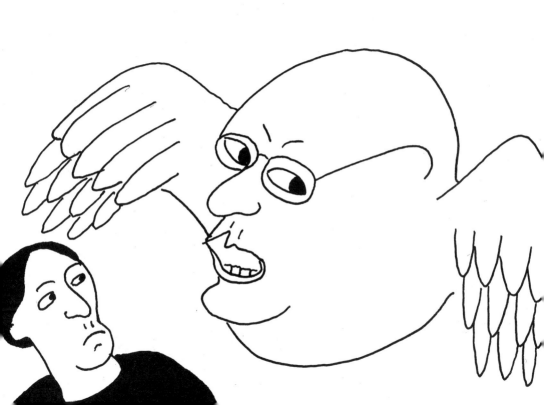

WHEN YOU START HAVING
THOUGHTS LIKE THESE,
YOU KNOW THAT

THE CHENEY WITHIN

HAS ARISEN.

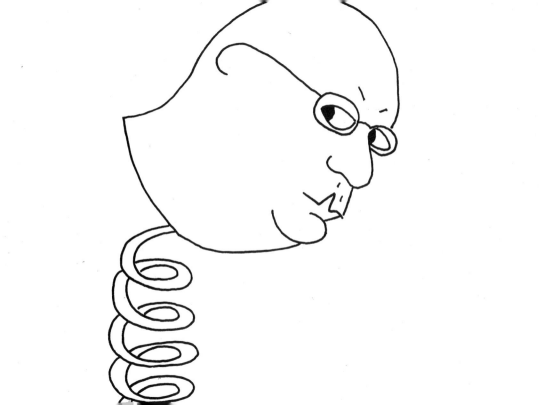

WHEN THIS HAPPENS,
YOU MUST NEVER TRY TO
SUPPRESS
THE
INNER CHENEY

BECAUSE
THE NEXT THING YOU KNOW...

HE'LL COME BACK AND
BITE YOU!

You MIGHT SAY...

"WELL THAT'S ALL WELL AND GOOD, THERE ARE PEOPLE OUT THERE WHO ARE **GREEDY** AND FULL OF **ILL WILL**

FOR THE PLANET, BUT

I'M NOT ONE OF THEM!

I WANT ONLY GOOD THINGS FOR THE PLANTS, THE ANIMALS AND THE HUMAN RACE."

IN THIS CASE, YOU MIGHT BE

IN A STATE OF **DENIAL.**

PEOPLE WHO PLAN TOO MUCH

PLANNING IS IMPORTANT, **BUT**
IT CAN BE TAKEN TO AN **EXTREME**
SOME PLANNING CAN BE UNHELPFUL.
EXAMPLES OF THIS ARE:

- PLANNING TO INVADE ANOTHER COUNTRY
- PLANNING TO WIPE OUT YOUR ENEMIES
- PLANNING TO WRECK THE ENVIRONMENT

SETTING BOUNDARIES

TELL YOUR INNER CHENEY:

"OKAY, YOU CAN DRILL FOR OIL IN YOSEMITE NATIONAL PARK BUT **NOT** THE GRAND CANYON"

It MAY BE THAT WHAT YOU NEED IS

VALIDATION.

SOMETIMES AGGRESSIVE ACTING OUT IS BASED ON THE NEED FOR ACKNOWLEDGEMENT. YOU MIGHT HAVE A **LOST CHILD COMPLEX,** AND NEED **INNER REGIME CHANGE.**

WALKING A ROAD
LESS TRAVELED

Recovery means asking for
what you need.

NAMING your addictive thought
patterns can be **TRANSFORMATIVE**
and set you firmly on the

PATH TO RECOVERY

THERAPY

Sometimes it's helpful to get one-on-one
Counseling in a SAFE ENVIRONMENT
to discuss your
PERSONAL PROBLEMS and FIXATIONS.

Your Counselor should point you towards a
HEALTHIER and MORE BALANCED
way of thinking.

SHARING OUR SURVIVOR STORIES

COMMUNICATING OUR STORIES TO A RECEPTIVE AND SUPPORTIVE AUDIENCE OF OUR PEERS CAN BRING HEALING AND COUNTER A SENSE OF ISOLATION

SUPPORT GROUPS

IT'S HELPFUL TO SURROUND YOURSELF WITH FELLOW PEERS, OR A **SOUL MATE** TO WORK ON **ISSUES** OF **INTIMACY.** THIS PERSON COULD BE:

- A FELLOW CEO WHO CHEATS THE COUNTRY OUT OF BILLIONS OF DOLLARS.
- SOMEONE WHO LIKES A PERFECT, CHEMICALLY TREATED WEED-FREE LAWN.

AFFIRMATIONS
(CHANGING THE INNER TAPES)

LOOK IN THE MIRROR, AND GENTLY
    REPEAT THESE PHRASES:

    " IT'S OKAY TO BE ME."
    " MAY I BE HAPPY."
    " MAY MY STOCK OPTIONS IN
HALLIBURTON SHOOT THROUGH THE ROOF."

INSTEAD OF GOING OUT AND

BLASTING AWAY

DEFENSELESS LITTLE CREATURES...

LEARN TO **LOVE**

THE ANIMALS,

AND PET THEM WHEN YOU CAN.

DIET

The food you eat can be a very important part of your spiritual path.

Instead of eating the usual

MEAT and POTATOES...

... TRY CHANGING THOSE
OLD FOOD HABITS,
AND SWITCH TO A
LIGHT VEGETARIAN
DIET.

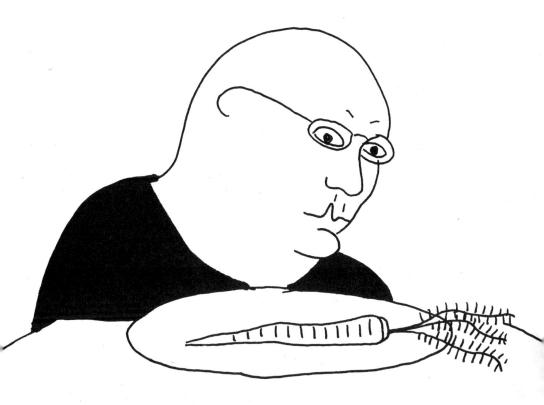

CREATIVE VISUALIZATION

FOCUS YOUR ATTENTION ON YOUR
THIRD EYE.

FILL YOUR MIND WITH A CALM,
BLUE LIGHT. IMAGINE UNICORNS
AND FAIRIES, AND

TRY NOT TO KILL THEM.

SMALL is BEAUTIFUL

You don't **NEED** to take over
the world.

Sometimes the smallest
things can be the most precious...

Like a hug or a flower.

YOGA

Yoga poses can lower blood pressure and provide a sense of well-being, and relieve stress buildup.

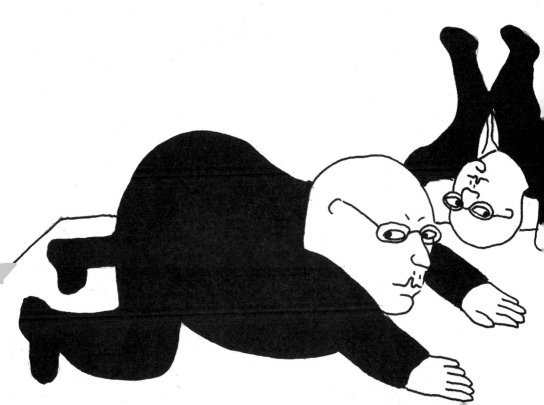

STORYTELLING AND CHANTING

EXPLORING MYTHOLOGY CAN OPEN US UP TO OUR OWN **HERO IDEALS.**

SOME MYTHS TO CONSIDER:

- WEAPONS OF MASS DESTRUCTION
- IMMINENT THREATS
- TIES TO TERRORIST GROUPS

HOBBIES

SHOCK and AWE your friends with your creativity.

Try projects like
       macrame and origami.

PAINT YOURSELF A PURPLE SUNSET

FOLLOWING THE **ARTIST'S WAY** CAN BE INSTRUMENTAL IN TRANSFORMING

YOUR **TOXIC ENERGY**

INTO WORKS OF

GREAT BEAUTY.

Join a Drum Circle

AWAKEN YOUR INNER FIRE

EXPRESS LATENT ENERGY AND
Commune with other men in a
PROTECTIVE HEALING SPACE

CREATE YOUR OWN ZEN GARDEN

instead of
planting INFORMATION
try
planting a GARDEN!

SOMETIMES YOU WILL FIND THAT
NONE OF THESE THINGS WORK.
MALEVOLENCE AND **GREED**
HAVE REACHED A CRESCENDO OF
EPIC PROPORTIONS.
IN THIS CASE, YOU MIGHT
BE IN A

CHENEY SHAME SPIRAL!

CRYSTALS

CRYSTALS PLACED IN SPECIFIC
LOCATIONS CAN CHANGE THE ENERGY
FIELD OF YOUR HOME ENVIRONMENT.

THEY CAN ACTUALLY TRANSFORM
THE **VIBRATIONAL
PATTERN**
OF YOUR **AURA.**

ESSENTIAL OILS

AROMATHERAPY CAN BE A VERY RELAXING WAY TO **LET GO.**

SOME COMPANIES THAT MAKE THESE ESSENTIAL OILS ARE:
- **EXXON**
- **CHEVRON**
- **MOBIL**

MEDITATION

DON'T JUST SIT THERE PLOTTING AND STRATEGIZING. EMPTY YOUR MIND, AND FILL YOUR HEART WITH **COMPASSION...**

NOT COMPASSIONATE CONSERVATISM.

SUBMIT TO THE

HIGHER POWER...

EVEN IF YOU THINK

YOU ARE THE HIGHER POWER

Finding a Sacred Space

A TRUST SPACE CAN BE A POWERFUL WAY FOR DEEP HEALING TO OCCUR. THIS SPACE COULD BE A KIND OF BUNKER OR BOMB SHELTER.

OR... perhaps a kind of **CRIB,** WHERE YOU CAN **LOCK** him away for a while, to keep him from doing any more **DAMAGE.**